CONTENTS

Trinity Mirror Media

Special Contributor:
Harry McLeish

Compiled by:
Vicky Andrews, Peter Grant, Ken Rogers
Design: Zoe Bevan
Liverpool Daily Post & Echo Image Archive:
Brian Johnston

Pictures copyright Liverpool Daily Post & Echo
and Harry McLeish.
With thanks to Stephen Guy of
Merseyside Maritime Museum

Business Development Director: Mark Dickinson
Executive Editor: Ken Rogers
Senior Editor: Steve Hanrahan
Editor: Paul Dove
Senior Art Editor: Rick Cooke
Trinity Mirror Media Marketing Executive: Claire Brown
Sales and Marketing Manager: Elizabeth Morgan
Sales and Marketing Assistant: Karen Cadman

Printed by Pensord

ISBN 978-1-906802-68-4

Last day at Laird's in 1983 – Harry McLeish
looks back on his 45-year career

LIFE OF A LAIRDSMAN

HARRY McLEISH, an ex-Ships Manager, is a character. He worked on some of the most celebrated vessels built in Britain since the Second World War. Here he talks to Peter Grant...

HARRY is a member of the Society of Authors; a lecturer; musician; naval and marine historian.

Call Harry what you want, he won't mind. But, at the end of the day, he wants to be remembered as a loyal LAIRDSMAN.

Harry's earliest memories are from the age of two when his father brought home a Hornby train set.

His eyes still focus now as strong as ever in 2011.

At the age of 90 they shine as brightly as they did during his 45-year career at the world famous shipyard, Cammell Laird.

A life that brought him a great deal of satisfaction, personally and professionally. And still does.

In those eyes you can see that whatever he did, he would give it 100 per cent.

"We lived at 168 County Road, Liverpool, over a chandler's shop," he says in the beautiful Crosby care home he lives in. Engineering clearly ran in the McLeish family – that train set fascinated his father.

"We had a round table so he put the track on it. My mother used to plonk me on a rug in front of a blazing fire and all the gang used to gather around, wind up the train, and it would whizz around."

That is one of his earliest recollections (he has millions of others – especially about ships and submarines).

"My father owned two chandler's shops. We were very 'well off' in those days."

Harry is (and always was) a stickler for detail, so much so that he has even produced limited edition ledgers of all the vessels he has ever worked on – more than 70 famous maritime names.

This Everton heights boy – raised in Bootle – knew instinctively that it would stand him in good stead for his later career. Instinct should be his middle name.

"I went to Venice Street school at the age of five until seven. It was there that I danced around the maypole and I also remember rocking horses." ➤

An aerial shot of the Cammell Laird shipyard at its peak

Harry pictured in 1946, and left, remembering the past – at home in Crosby

It was there he also nurtured a life-long love of art, music, and sport, especially football, as well as the cinema: "My mother used to take me in the afternoon to see Ben Hur."

Harry has always had an incredible imagination and a photographic memory.

"My father had taught me copper-plate writing at a very early age, and also calligraphy. This was to follow me all my life because, in latter years, when I retired, I used to teach calligraphy in the local schools."

Harry was also an accomplished artist – from the age of ten.

"When I was at Bedford Road School, I was commended on my 'still life' work. I also drew pictures of Everton and Liverpool players.

"I had a little bit of help, though, with my drawing, from cartoonists like George Green. I used to cut his famous cartoons out of the Liverpool Echo."

For a man who was to climb to the top of his mast in the shipbuilding world, Harry regards his own formative education with a self-effacing charm.

"I didn't pass the scholarship and my dad had to go down to the education offices.

"They said that they only accepted two paying scholars a year in the grammar school. I reckon my dad must have emptied his wallet, because I finished up in the grammar school. He made sure that we had a good education.

"My brother David was more educated than me, because I must admit, I was 'thick' at school. Not what you would call a good scholar."

But he had talent as a violin player, organist and singer. When his Welsh mother, Margaret, forced him into the church choir he knew he would never look back. She was delighted when her son joined the Cammell Laird Male Voice Choir.

Says Harry: "I worked on the engines of the submarines on the plateau in the main engine shop.

"There was a huge cyclindrical fire there made of steel and we used to gather around it in the winter to eat our sarnies. Some of the men were from Wales and they would start to hum and gradually this sound swelled into the singing of Welsh hymns and songs.

"I would join in because I was taught them by my mother."

Young Harry was always a good talker – and a great listener. But what about a career?

"I don't think I knew what job I wanted to do when I was at secondary school. After three weeks in the A stream studying Latin and the like, a letter was sent to my mother saying: 'This lad shows no aptitude for studying anything, so we are putting him in the joinery class'.

"Now, that was the best thing they ever did because whatever I made, I had to draw out to size and give it to the teacher. I could never settle down to do exams.

"I hated them", he chuckles.

"So I winded up in the joinery class which I enjoyed very much. ➤

Harry's wife Sheila. Above, brothers-in-arms, Harry in his Home Guard uniform alongside Naval Officer David

Scaling new heights in the yard in 1960.
Below left, the boilership and right, the power station

View from Tranmere Hill, Birkenhead in 1950, as
Ark Royal is ready for launching from Cammell Laird

The fifth ship of the Royal Navy to bear the name HMS Coventry, a Sea Dart missile destroyer, launched at Cammell Laird in June 1974

➤ "One day I proudly ran home with a bundle of drawings under my arm..."

When he went in for the school certificate for a preliminary exam he failed it so they put him down a year, and he failed again – although he passed math, so they put him in the Upper Sixth. Then he set sail for the real world.

"I had to start looking for a job then. I was sixteen and a half."

Harry spent six months looking for employment.

"I'd go around to banks. I would send letters.

"Companies would admire my lovely handwriting and I would get an interview.

BIRKENHEAD BECKONS

"I was fed up one day and decided to cross the river to Birkenhead and I got off on Woodside. I thought that I'd try and get a job with a skill like my dad's as a boiler-maker.

"He was a very practical man – a good engineer.

"He'd sailed as a third engineer on the Aquitania.

"So I was walking up Woodside. It was a bitter January morning in 1938. I was kicking a tin can up the road until I saw a sign saying 'Grayson and Clover' and I thought I'd try my luck there.

"I was always smartly dressed and a good interviewee. I went in and there was a commissionaire. I asked if there were any jobs and he said: 'Clear off'. And in the background was this fella who asked what the problem was? He told the commissionaire he had no right to chase me off and I was put in his office and given a cup of tea. And then he gave me a letter. He was very friendly with a man at another place called...Cammell Laird.

"He told me to pop down to this shipyard and show him this letter. Well, I did, and when I got there he said: 'Well, you went to a grammar school, surely you've got a certificate?'

Polaris submarine HMS Renown slides into the Mersey in 1967, with proud Cammell Laird workers riding high on her back and thousands of others cheering her on

"And I said no. I was 'too thick', but I did show him a certificate I had in my pocket.

"He looked at it and said: 'Start next Tuesday'.

"That certificate was for swimming half a mile at Balliol Road baths. And that's how I got into Cammell Laird's. I stayed there for 45 years. I wanted to be a boiler maker but I was made one better – a fitter."

So that's how Harry McLeish started a life of adventure, working hard, being promoted and never looking back.

"I walked into the engine shop for the first time on February 3, 1938 and was just amazed. I looked up to the roof but you couldn't see it because the smoke was so thick.

"During the war, one S-Class submarine went through there a month. They bore the brunt of the war. We made those engines from nothing."

Each day he would leave the family home in Asser Road, Clubmoor, that he shared with his parents and younger brother, David, and take the tram from Townsend Lane to Liverpool James Street station, and then the train to Green Lane station, Birkenhead.

"I would get up at 5.30am and set off with blue overalls under one arm and a tin-box under the other with my sandwiches and conny-onny tea, which I had in a tin beaker when we got to work."

"Outside the station, there would be hundreds of men milling and then you heard the 7.25 buzzer and ➤

Anguished relatives at Cammell Laird receive the false hope that the submarine Thetis is safe in 1939

you ran like mad to clock-on in the engine shop.

"I started off filing at the bench. We used to file off big spanners for the tail end of propellers. One day, in 1938, we learnt that the great submarine was about to be launched – The Thetis.

"I went cap-in-hand to ask if I could go to the launch."

TRAGEDY OF THE THETIS

Harry had only been at the yard a short while yet he sensed these were momentous times.

He will not forget waving off that submarine – not realising then that he, too, was entering history.

"It was a massive occasion as the Thetis was the pride of the Royal Navy. The submarine was the first of its class, I was in awe watching it go as I was only a 16-year-old apprentice at the time."

He would be there again on June 1, 1939. By then, the Thetis had been completed in the yard's fitting-out basin and was about to leave Birkenhead for her sea trials. The catastrophe which followed has been the subject of books, numerous articles, documentaries and dramas, as well as an official inquiry.

On board the Thetis were 103 men – 99 of whom died after she dived into 180ft of water in Liverpool Bay, some 15 miles off Llandudno. The dead comprised 68 Royal Navy personnel, 24 Cammell Laird workers, four observers from other yards, a Mersey pilot and the two caterers, who had provided lunch on board.

Right, the submarine Thetis. Below, Harry lays a wreath at the Thetis Memorial at Holyhead, Anglesey

Harry shakes his head as if remembering yesterday, then, he says, looking away:

"I reckon it was doomed before it left Birkenhead."

During his time at Cammell Laird, Harry also worked on the Thunderbolt, and the Trident, and the Talisman. He says: "They were the T Class boats."

And Harry is proud all over again when he talks of the Ark Royal, the best in the world.

"I used to specialise in pipe work and fittings and auxiliary machinery. We used to sail out form Gorock, right out to sea, and do the trials and come back again. I used to sleep on board. All of us had nice bunks because it wasn't crewed up."

June 1954 was extra special for Harry McLeish.

"When asked what was the happiest day of my life,

apart from my marriage to my lovely Sheila, of course, I would say June 25, 1954, because that was the day the lads I worked with had saved up for a present for me. I showed my mother and father my bowler hat."

Bowled over, Harry was now management. That same lad who had kicked a can up the street looking for a job had been promoted at 33 years of age.

That other 'special' occasion was his marriage to his beloved Sheila.

"I sang the Bells of St Mary's when we got married.

"It's a very appropriate song when you come home from the sea. Sheila and I had no children, but we had a marvellous marriage. I met her at a Scottish Caledonian dance. We were married for 56 years until she sadly died." ➤

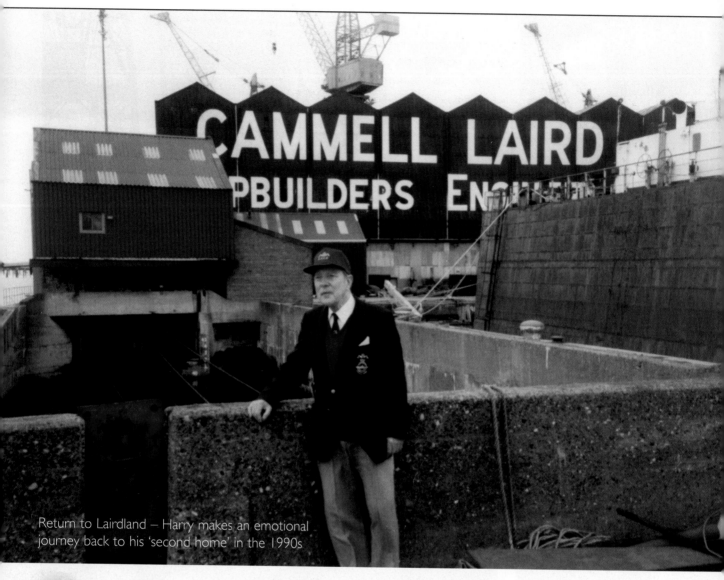

Return to Lairdland – Harry makes an emotional journey back to his 'second home' in the 1990s

➤ From his wonderfully evocative room in Crosby, with pictures, drawings and certificates covering every inch of space, Harry tells me that he and Sheila travelled and loved life together on and off shore, when he retired from Cammell Laird.

ONCE A LAIRDSMAN...

"When I became a manager at Cammell Laird's they used to send me out with slides to do lectures at local schools on all the ships they'd built. I brought hundreds of lads into Cammell Laird's. I even used to take half a day from my own annual leave holiday to go around schools. I was, and still am, that proud of the place. It was amazing how the lads in Laird's all got on together and went on to greater things. One time I was at a plumbers' ball at the Adelphi Hotel.

"There were 750 people there and this very smartly-dressed man came up to me and said: 'I remember you, Harry, you had two sugars in your tea.' He'd done very well. There were no end of personalities and the Camaraderie was excellent."

Harry was and still is a Lairdsman through and through. Ask him his favourite vessels and he can reel them all off. The Lady of Landsdowne, the Astronomer, Naworth, HMS Liverpool, HMS Coventry...

"I was very proud to be a Lairdsman because I had a very happy time there. I never ever got bored – I served my time there, no two days were alike."

Given his chance would he do it all again?

Harry, the author of a book called The Sunset Over Cherbourg about the SS Alabama, replies with a sparkle:

"No, I would go back to the wooden shipbuilding days, when they built the American Civil War raider Alabama, which my book was based on. I am 90 but my ambition is to see it made into a film."

Then sipping a mug of tea, he says, looking at his own hand-crafted model of the Alabama and his painting of the Thetis on the Wall: "You know they could have made the Titanic at Cammell Laird. They made The Alabama after all.

"I have always lived in high hopes.

"I was . . . I am, a Lairdsman."

Harry joined former Cammell Laird workers at an emotional thanksgiving at the vast construction hall in 1993. The ecumenical service, to mark the closure of the shipyard, was led by the Bishop of Birkenhead, the Rt Rev Michael Langrish

THE BIRKENHEAD DREAM

For over 200 years the vision of a mercantile giant – a zest for life and innovation – has towered over the River Mersey. HARRY McLEISH brings a remarkable story to life...

CAMMELL Laird is a world famous brand name, as well known in ports all over the globe as it is along the docklands of Merseyside.

'Wooden ships and iron men' – that fine old sea phrase of the celebrated 'Clipper Ships' era – seems to best describe the great British shipbuilding and engineering firm that still stands proudly on the Birkenhead waterfront, as much a Mersey icon in its own way as the Three Graces at the Pier Head.

The remarkable men who founded and pioneered this business challenged both the Admiralty and the mighty insurance giants Lloyds of London, along the way in the 19th century battle to build the new iron ships that would replace their old historic counterparts. And a battle it was, make no mistake about it.

The story began in 1810, the year William Laird first came to Liverpool. Then 30 years old, he was a short,

thick set Scotsman with penetrating blue eyes and an enormous zest for business. His task was to build up an order book for his father's Greenock ropeworks. Failing in this but quite undaunted, he plunged into several other projects.

He became a Director for two shipping companies, bought a sugar house and started an agency for the famous Watts' Steam Engine.

His boundless energy and restless spirit also convinced him that Birkenhead too could become one of Britain's great ports. So he began to purchase land on the Birkenhead side of the river with the two-pronged idea of building a harbour and cutting a canal across the Wirral Peninsula to the River Dee, which in those days was much safer than the Mersey which had shifting mud banks.

William Laird's first slice of Cheshire land lay on the north side of Wallasey Pool, on one side of which was the modern jetty named Vittoria Wharf. His scheme was very ambitious, so he began to look for financial partners. But reluctant to see his land lying idle during the search and following his wily Scottish sense of values, he built a boiler works there which he named the Birkenhead Iron Works.

Although his plans to build up Birkenhead as a port collapsed, Laird did succeed in securing a firm industrial foothold in Wirral, even building a town for his workers. It was a fine town, with an elegant square in the middle. There were gaslights and every home had its own water supply.

It was a far cry from the unplanned squalor that the Industrial Revolution had produced elsewhere. To William Laird's everlasting credit was his contribution of the dignity of labour, which more than established him as a great man.

In 1828, when the Birkenhead Iron Works was four years old, two significant events occurred. The first concerned William Laird's son John, a solicitor by profession, who joined the firm. The second was the company's first ship building order – a 90 foot 'Lighter' built of iron for the Irish Inland Steam Navigation Company. She was completed in 1829 and, after a trial floating, was dismantled, shipped across to Ireland and then reassembled by Lairdsmen. ➤

John Laird, son of William Laird who founded Birkenhead Iron Works in 1824

Mr Laird's shipbuilding yard, from an 1856 edition of the Illustrated London News

➤ The vessel named 'Wye' was such a success that orders for two more followed.

The next year, 1830, firmly established the company as shipbuilders. The main factor was another order from the same Irish company for a 113 foot long paddle steamboat, to be named Lady Lansdowne. At William Laird's suggestion she was equipped with water-tight bulkheads, an almost unheard of practice at the time.

Indeed, the battle of iron versus wood was now joined. Even though ships had been made of wood since the dawn of history and the Royal Navy, the most powerful in the world, had become to be known as The Wooden Walls of England, these ships had much to condemn them.

Their timbers came in short lengths, which had to be joined together. Every joint was a weakness. The addition of boilers and engines put an impossible strain on the hulls, increasing the risk. The thickness of the timbers themselves also took up valuable cargo space. As if this was not enough, the suppliers of timber at home were running short.

Forest after forest was stripped of trees, and farmers – finding more profit in crops – were not replanting them. Consequently, the timber, much of it inferior, had to be imported. Iron, on the other hand, was plentiful in Britain and seemed an ideal material for ship building. William John Laird decided the future was in iron ships.

In the ranks of the anti-iron faction were government departments, underwriters and private ship owners, all of whom provided the stiffest opposition. To combat this, Laird plunged into scientific research and, in 1837, invited the Astronomer Royal, Professor Airey, to carry out tests aboard their latest iron ship, The Rainbow. Professor Airey's research produced the first gleam of hope and finally led to the acceptance of what is known as 'Deviation'.

Even while the scientific investigations were being made, the pioneering spirit of the young shipyard continued. In 1834, it completed the John Randolph, the first iron ship to be built for a North American ship owner. Three years later it finished the then largest iron ship of her day, the Rainbow, for the General Steam Navigation Company. The following year, in 1838, it turned out the first screw driven ship to cross the Atlantic, the Robert F. Stockton. Another ship from the yard, L'Egyptien, was the first iron steam ship to make the passage from England to Alexandria, and thence up the Nile.

The firm also helped the East India Company to establish a short sea route to India. This was by ship to the Eastern end of the Mediterranean, then over land by camel caravan to the Persian Gulf where travellers re-embarked on the Laird-build 'Euphrates' for the last lap of their journey. It should be said straight away that this was not where the Cammell in the eventual Cammell Lairds title came from! More of that later.

By 1838, the yard had built seven ships and on the surface things seemed to be progressive and as lively as anyone could have wished for, but the iron ship was not sufficiently established.

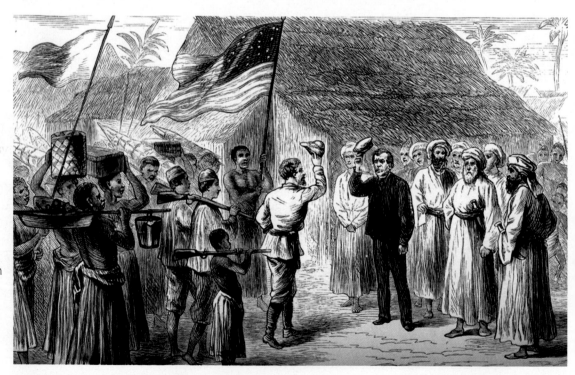

Dr Livingstone, I presume? MacGregor Laird met the legendary African explorer and influenced him to visit Birkenhead where he viewed the plans for the famous ship 'Ma Roberts'

The Nemesis steamer destroying Chinese war bunks, in the Canton River. From a sketch by the Hon. East India Company, circa 1840

The diehards stiffened their defences and the Laird orders became fewer and fewer. A slump swept across Birkenhead, the gas was cut off, and weeds began to push their way through the pavements. It would be 12 years before the 'Golden Age' finally arrived.

THE EXPLORER AND ADVENTURER IN THE LAIRD FAMILY

The slump also closed down a small sister yard on the Liverpool bank which MacGregor Laird, John's brother, had started in 1832. Though in existence for only a few years its output was extremely varied, ranging from steamships for the P & O Line, to 'Lighters' and also vessels for African rivers.

MacGregor Laird, it would seem, was more adventurer than shipbuilder. He spent a good deal of time on several trips to Africa as both explorer, and businessman. There are several, sometimes harrowing, tales of his experiences there. But he succeeded in founding the Africa Steam Navigation Company (taken over by Elder Dempster after his death in 1861).

MacGregor met the legendary African explorer Dr Livingstone, and influenced him to visit Birkenhead where he viewed the plans on the drawing board for the famous 'Ma Roberts'.

MacGregor also had a town named after the Laird family (Lairdstown). Livingstone stayed with the Lairds at 63 Hamilton Square.

THE OPIUM WARS AND THE DEVIL SHIP

Meanwhile, business in Birkenhead was anything but brisk. In spite of the successes, the Admiralty in particular stubbornly held out against iron and steam.

There were claims that Paddles were vulnerable to cannon shot, and that screw-propped ships could not be steered.

John Laird, however, was not without ammunition to use on the Whitehall pundits. In 1839, four gunboats built by the yard for the East India Company were diverted to China to support the naval force during the first of the Opium Wars. One of them, The Nemesis, the first iron ship to round the Cape of Good Hope, became the terror of the Chinese.

She was so successful against them they dubbed her the 'Devil Ship'.

LAIRDS TAKE ON THE MIGHT OF THE ADMIRALTY

By the 1840s, however, many must have believed Laird's had failed. The firm's order books were virtually blank. The fine young town of Birkenhead ➤

Captain Raphael Semmes, Alabama's commanding officer, standing by his ship's 110-pounder rifled gun during her visit to Capetown in August 1863. Photograph from US Naval Historical Center

> lay stripped by a slump. Even though that year the yard built the first iron ship owned by the British Government, the 113 foot Dover, plus four gunboats for the Royal Navy, this construction was not enough. The Admiralty still persisted with its argument that iron ships were only fit for rivers, not short sea voyages. Steam power was only used for getting in and out of harbours. Once at sea, captains had orders to look to their sails.

John Laird decided the only way to discredit their Lordships' argument was by practical proof.

He took a chance and built a ship 'on spec'. She was a 187 foot frigate propelled by paddle wheels, Stubbornness still prevailed and the ship was rejected and eventually sold to Mexico.

As the 'Guadalupe' she won several encounters in Mexico's war against Texas.

Small rays of light occasionally managed to pierce the reactionary fog. Iron, steam driven ships won so much acclaim that one day during the 1840s the Admiralty placed an order for five iron frigates. One of them 'The Birkenhead', was entrusted to Laird.

Again, the 'wooden wall' diehards raised such a clamour that the Birkenhead's guns were removed and she was converted into a troop ship.

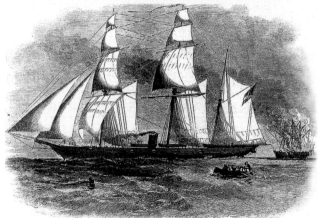

Above, CSS Alabama, from 'Harper's Weekly' in 1862. Below, iron steam-driven ship The Birkenhead is lost on the Cape of Good Hope in 1852

She sailed to Cork, where soldiers embarked for South East Africa. Just after she rounded the Cape of Good Hope, she struck a submerged rock. The story of heroism and discipline known as the 'Birkenhead Drill' which attended her sinking has since become a chapter of history.

THE 'ALABAMA' BECAME A CONFEDERATE RAIDER

Another Laird built warship to make the mid-nineteenth century headlines was the Confederate raider 'Alabama' that was heavily involved in the American War of Independence. Strangely enough, this was a wooden ship, built in 1863 as a commercial raider for the Confederate Navy.

All manner of attempts were made to prevent her delivery, which was accomplished by the fact that the ship did not return to Birkenhead after her final trials.

The guests were put ashore by tug at a point on the Welsh coast and she sailed off the Azores where the owner's crew took over.

THE CHANGE THAT TRANSFORMED LAIRD'S FORTUNES AND RESHAPED MERSEYSIDE'S DESTINY

A change took place on Merseyside at the beginning of the 1850s. It was generated by the removal of the Navigation Laws. This compelled British owners to look at their ships with a more critical eye. The few iron ships that were then in service had proved themselves to be much stronger than their wooden counterparts.

In 1846, for example, Brunel's famous iron ship the 'Great Britain' went ashore on the Irish coast. When she was finally refloated a year later, only minor repairs were necessary. This was the sort of proof that appealed to the pockets of imagination of every ship owner. As a result there were more orders for iron ships, Laird's speciality.

In 1856 Lloyds finally acknowledged the existence of iron merchantmen by issuing specifications for them. In that year, there occurred an event which was to reshape the destiny of Merseyside. ➤

Liverpool's bustling waterfront as depicted in the painting 'The Port of Liverpool 1873' by Samuel Walters, on display at Merseyside Maritime Museum

The morning commute across the River Mersey in 1886, taken from the Illustrated London News

➤ The Birkenhead Docks were still unfinished and something had to be done. It took the form of an Act of Parliament which ruled that they should be taken over and completed by Liverpool.

The Mersey Docks and Harbour Board was formed in 1858 and John Laird was appointed to it as a government nominee. John Laird retired from the shipyard in 1861, but he returned to public life in 1863 when he became the first Member of Parliament for Birkenhead.

He died in 1874, by which time the control of the firm had passed to his sons William, John, and Henry.

GOLDEN AGE WHEN 'A LAIRD'S YARD WITHOUT A WARSHIP WAS LIKE A CHURCH WITHOUT A STEEPLE'

The Laird yard grew in size with the arrival of the 'Golden Age'. More people were employed and ship building became a much more specialised business. There were plenty of orders to be had, but competition was increasing. That old enemy, the Clyde, lay alert to the north. Nothing pleased Clydeside more than to snatch orders from Merseyside.

What kind of facilities did Lairds have to build ships? During the middle of the nineteenth century, the premises were confined to what is known as the North Yard. In it were five graving docks, two of them over 400 feet long, and four building slips. Two of the slips had shed roofing over them. About this time, an engine shop was added.

From the earliest days, the firm known as Cammell Laird & Company was noted for its pioneering approach to ship building. In the second half of the nineteenth century, it also became noted for its approach to the ships themselves. How the company, in 1903, merged with that of John Cammell will come later. In the second half of the nineteenth century, Lairds also became noted for its approach to the ships themselves. A Laird-built ship invariably had very fine lines and an unusually fast turn of speed. As a result, between 1870 and 1900, 270 ships came from the Birkenhead slipways, among them the liners for the Cunard Company, P & O, Inman's International Line, and 16 ships for the Pacific Steam Packet Company.

Such swift, luxurious and shapely vessels inevitably attracted the attention of wealthy men.

W.K. Vanderbilt, the American millionaire, placed one on order for the 1,823 ton (gross) 'Valient'. Not a

Above, The Hibernia under repair at Laird's Graving Docks in 1861. Below, the battleship Royal Oak was launched from Laird's in 1892

piece of brass was allowed to be seen on the yacht. All fittings normally made from this substance were to be made of 'approved metal in imitation silver'.

Meanwhile, at the Admiralty, the last barriers of prejudice against ironclads and screws crumbled. In 1863 a full reconstruction programme for the Royal Navy was approved of which, however, Lairds received only a small part. Undaunted, they kept trying and by 1885 were recognised as builders of warships on a grand scale.

Between then and 1900, the yard built four of the largest ships in the British Navy – the Royal Oak (15,150 tons), Mars (14,900 tons), the Glory (12,950 tons) and the Exmouth (14,000 tons). A popular saying at the time stated: "Laird's yard without a warship is like a church without a steeple."

During "The Turbulent Years" of 1890-1900, Lairds built 71 ships, 46 of which were warships or naval auxiliaries. Other shipyards were building liners and large cargo ships. These orders by-passed Birkenhead because the yard was not big enough to handle them. Its largest dry dock was only 4440 feet long. The firm had to expand, but where was the land to come from?

The existing yard was tightly restricted, being

1908 map showing Clover's Graving Docks (Grayson Rollo and Clover, later Western Ship Repairers Limited) and Birkenhead Iron Works to the south of Monk's Ferry

confined between the Mersey on one side and the streets of Birkenhead on the other. At the northern end, the way was blocked by Grayson's Yard and Monks Ferry. To the south, there were the newly built headquarters of the Royal Mersey Yacht Club, a row of large private houses, and a small shipyard owned by Messrs John Jones & Sons.

In 1900, Laird Bros and John Jones & Sons combined to form the Tranmere Bay Development Company. The Royal Mersey Yacht Club, not unnaturally angry, and the owners of the private houses were asked to leave to make room for the expansion programme.

The enlarged yard, capable of building the biggest ships imaginable at that time, had a total area of 98.5 acres. The 15-acre fitting-out Basin was the largest private wet dock in Britain. Six new slipways were laid down, the biggest to take a ship 1,000 feet long. Two new graving docks were built and the excavated materials were used for land reclamation. Vast engine and boiler shops were also added, as were a complete railway system and heavy capacity cranes.

AGE OF THE BIG MERGER

The world famous Cammell Laird name is born

MEANWHILE, William, John, and Henry Laird had all died, and their places at the top were taken by their sons, J. MacGregor Laird (son of John and senior partner), Roy. M. Laird and J.W.P. Laird.

In 1900 the firm became a public company known as Laird Bros & Company Ltd.

The age of the big merger having arrived, three years later the firm became Cammell Laird (1903). The large Sheffield steel producing firm of Charles Cammell & Company Ltd, founded in 1828 by Charles Cammell, joined with Lairds and this was applauded by the Admiralty.

The general idea was that one group of companies would now be able to see a job right through from raw materials to finished product. At the time of the merger, Cammell was also part owner of an ordnance works in Coventry, coalmines, iron ore mines and smelting works at Worthington, a file factory in Odessa, Russia, a steel and iron works at Penistone, and two steelworks, Cyclops and Grimesthorpe, in Sheffield. This was now a giant business and J. MacGregor Laird became chairman of the new organisation, Cammell Laird & Co. Ltd.

All seemed well, but financial difficulties and setbacks during the lean years of 1908-1908 might well have destroyed a company with less resilience than Cammell Laird. Though it survived, the period did unfortunately remove a Laird from heading the firm, and no Laird has been at the head since.

Dr. Francis Elgar F.R.S. replaced J. MacGregor Laird. Upon Dr. Elgar's death in 1910, his place was taken by young financier, William Lionel Hichens. ➤

"This was now a giant business and J MacGregor Laird became chairman of the the new organisation"

It was hard, heavy work in the shipyard

Construction and repair, a scene in Cammell Laird
taken by Edward Chambré Hardman in 1931

Battleship HMS Rodney, completed in 1927, makes her last voyage to the shipbreakers yard in Scotland, 1948

SHADOW OF WAR PROVES AN IRONIC BOOST FOR FORTUNES

Starting in 1909, things began to look up, almost as if anticipating World War I.

From the Admiralty came orders for cruisers, destroyers, a 23,090 ton battleship HMS Audacious, and a Floating Dock.

The latter is one of the legends of Cammell Laird. She was designed to lift 32,000 tons and was the largest in the world. Her length was 640 feet and a special building slip, from which she could be floated, had to be made.

The war years naturally inspired a tremendous demand for ships. Amongst the famous Birkenhead built vessels and submarines was the cruiser HMS Chester, one of the heroes of Jutland. But the yard made an even more significant contribution to the war effort. This was the realm of Boiler Design. The boilers of the day just could not stand the high demands of World War I naval warfare.

After several boiler explosions, Cammell Laird was invited by the Admiralty to find a solution. The company's chief draughtsman solved the problem

H·M·36 KNOT TORPEDO BOAT DESTROYER 'SWIFT.'

to the Admiralty's complete satisfaction. As a result, the yard fitted over 50 warships with the new type of boiler.

The inevitable post war slump that hit ship building after November, 1918, did not overly distress the company. It was authorised to complete HMS Rodney and in addition obtained several merchant tonnage orders.

Two of these were noteworthy. The first was the 17,750 ton passenger line De Grasse, and the second was the Fullagar, the first all-welded merchantman built for the Anchor Brocklebank Line.

Ocean liner SS De Grasse, 1924

The Fullager, the first all-welded merchantman
built for the Anchor Brocklebank Line in 1920

THE LARGEST SHIP EVER TO BE LAUNCHED ON THE MERSEY

Top management changes at the time were equally noteworthy. Mr Robert Stewart Johnson (later Sir Robert), for many years a Director of Workman Clerk, joined the firm in 1920 and two years later he was made Managing Director. He was probably one of the most dynamic personalities to ever govern the fortunes of a shipyard.

What others saw as a calamity, he regarded as a challenge – even an opportunity. He chose the middle 1920s, for example, when the conditions in the shipbuilding industry were comparatively quiet and costs low, to carry out a yard modernisation programme.

Despite his great efforts, by 1931 the order book at Birkenhead was reduced to a solitary ship on the slipways. The big slump was on! Then, in 1935, came the order for HMS Ark Royal, the first Royal Navy vessel to be designed as an aircraft carrier. Costing £3,000,000, she was the largest ship ever to be launched on the Mersey.

She was the vessel that, in truth, prepared the yard for the tremendous task placed upon it by World War II.

Cammell Laird contributed much to Britain's Second World War ship building efforts. Many of the ships built at Birkenhead became household names. The Ark Royal, Prince of Wales, and Rodney all helped in the sinking of Germany's famous Bismark.

The Achilles was one of the cruisers responsible for the fat of another legendary German vessel, the Graf Spee. The destroyer Hardy led the attack at the first battle of Narvich.

The Prince of Wales carried the Prime Minister, Winston Churchill, to his historic meeting with President Franklin D. Roosevelt. The sloop Kite destroyed no fewer than six U-Boats. The submarine Talisman completed a cruise of eleven months, travelling 26,213 miles without a defect.

And the submarine Thrasher saw two VC's won on board.

In all, Cammell Laird built 106 fighting ships during those six fateful years of the war – an average of one every 20 days.

The launch of HMS Ark Royal in 1938

Ark Royal leaving Cammell Laird's shipyard, guided by a gaggle of Cock tugs past the Pier Head for Gladstone dry dock, in March, 1938

Mauretania the Second was much-loved by Merseysiders – they affectionately called her 'Maurie'. More than 50,000 shipyard workers, relatives and officials gathered for the launch in 1938. Above, Cammell Laird workers build the engines

From his office suite in the Cunard
Building on Liverpool's waterfront,
Cunard White Star's chairman Sir Percy
Bates virtually watched Mauretania II
being built across the river. She was
the third Cunarder to be built in the
company's own backyard

OFF'   166267
NETT REG TONS 19495 100

FROM WARSHIPS
TO MERCHANTMEN

Throughout its history, the shipyard at Birkenhead was noted for its versatility

TO switch production virtually overnight when the Second World War ended, from warships to merchantmen, was a feat requiring a great deal of flexibility. Ship owners of all kinds needed new vessels, some passenger, some cargo, others oil tankers.

The Royal Navy also "chipped in" with its order for the second aircraft carrier to be named Ark Royal. She was launched by HM Queen Elizabeth on 3rd May, 1950, and was completed in 1955.

The Royal visitor returned for another historic occasion in June 1959, when she launched the 30,000-ton Windsor Castle in brilliant sunshine. Queen Elizabeth told the crowds at the launching ceremony she was glad to be back again. She said: "The Windsor Castle bears a name symbolic of the traditions of our country and it is fitting that a seafaring nation should, even in this age of air travel, continue to build fine ships which would ply between the countries of our Commonwealth."

The Windsor Castle was the largest passenger liner built on Merseyside and the biggest to enter the South Africa service. ➤

Windsor Castle offered luxury accommodation for 880 passengers with first class public rooms, recreation spaces and a sun deck

HM Queen Elizabeth (the Queen Mother) launches Windsor Castle in 1959

Windsor Castle was the largest passenger liner to be launched at a British shipyard since the Queen Elizabeth in 1938. From the Liverpool side of the Mersey, crowds of people were able to see the launch from the Pier Head

Princess Alexandra launches HMS Devonshire, the Royal Navy's first guided missile destroyer in 1960

A county class destroyer of 4,000 tons, Devonshire was the first operational Royal Naval vessel to be fitted with stabilisers. Weapons included seaslug and seacat guided missiles

➤ Cammell Laird's concern with ships for the Royal Navy Line, was far from over. Not far from the slipway where the Windsor Castle was born in 1959, a revolutionary new ship was built a year later at the very start of the 1960s. HMS Devonshire was Britain's first guided missile ship.

Cammell Laird always demonstrated real enterprise when looking ahead to an extensive reconstruction and modernisation programme. On 17 April, 1962, Her Royal Highness, Princess Alexandra of Kent G.C.V.O., was present for the completion of the first phase of a great new dry dock, aptly named Princess Dock. No. 5 dry dock was extended to 950 feet.

With the vast increase in the size of modern vessels, ever larger docks had become necessary for their servicing and repair. Princess Dock had been designed to take the largest ships envisaged at that time, and provision was made for further extension.

To make way for the dock's construction – which called for the excavation of close on half a million tons of material – it was necessary to obtain the permission of the Ecclesiastical Authorities in order to move the disused cemetery of the parish church of St. Mary's, Birkenhead. It was also necessary to demolish some of the older shipyard offices, and to take in parts of three of the older streets of the town.

Like the rest of this great and historic ship yard, the new dock was equipped with the most up to date plant and ancillary services. The sliding arc gate was probably one of the largest of its type in the world.

The galleries on each side of the dock provided exceptionally comprehensive services for vessels using the dock, including compressed air, steam, salt water for ballasting, and fresh water, plus pipelines for discharging bunker oil, and electric power from two sub-stations, as well as the controls for the fully automated bilge blocks.

Floodlight towers would light the top deck, and the deck interior was lit from beneath the gallery canopies. The dock pumps operated from the Control Room at the head of the dock, and these could empty the dock in four hours. Flooding-up took about two hours.

This magnificent new dock would now play its part in serving efficiently and economically the next ships in the story as the city of Liverpool across the river began to throb to a different type of beat with The Beatles and Mersey Sound about to rock the world.

Princess Alexandra was invited to launch the cruiser HMS Devonshire, in 1960, seen here at the yard with the chairman R W Johnson. The Princess was back the following year for the opening of Princess Dock, pictured right. The ceremony marked the completion of the first phase of reconstruction and modernisation of the shipyard

Finishing touches are put to a steam catapult on
the flight deck of the Ark Royal, known among
pilots as the 'hot ride', in February 1955

Firemen at work on the riggers' shop fire in 1962.
It was Birkenhead's biggest fire for many years

Seated at the conference table with Mr G Moss,
managing director of Cammell Laird; Mr R Johnson,
chairman; and Mr M Wyatt, general manager, in 1967

The pump house in 1964, showing the 60" and 84" valves, pumps, motors and one of the 1250 HP diesel engines

Part of the great work of reconstruction at Cammell Laird in 1962, illustrating the way in which the new dock was built in two halves, linked by a tunnel, and then turned into a single entity by the removal of the central roadway

Taking a break –
Laird workers,
Will Rimmer,
Walter Green,
Sid Jones, Albert
Griffin, Alan Jones
and Billy Vaughan,
in 1969

Below, a 200 ton
pressure vessel
is lifted onto low
loaders in the
boiler shop at
Cammell Laird in
1967. The vessel
was to be used as
a CO2 absorber
at the Shell-Star
Fertilizer Plant at
Ince Marches, near
Ellesmere Port

ARK ROYAL – FLAGSHIP OF THE MERSEY

Giant wave for pride of the Royal Navy

MORE than 50,000 people watched as Queen Elizabeth (the Queen Mother) launched the British Navy's fourth Ark Royal on May 3, 1950.

It was the first time that a ship built on Merseyside had been launched by a Queen of England. As the new Ark Royal glided into the water, a flight of 30 aircraft gave a Royal salute and guns fired from the deck of the new vessel.

There were thousands in the shipyard itself, one stand alone accommodating 4,000 specially invited guests. After the religious ceremony led by the Bishop of Chester, the three choirs of St Mary's Parish Church, St Luke's Church and the Cammell Laird Male Voice Choir, sang hymns. Then the Queen stepped forward and named the ship Ark Royal and wished all who sail in her "God speed."

She took the be-ribboned bottle of Empire wine firmly in her hand and it crashed on the bow of the vessel. It was a perfect launch.

As the bow reached the end of the slipway it dipped gracefully. Workmen standing on the edge of the flight deck waved to the Queen, who waved back.

Crowds had gathered from early in the morning to get a good vantage point to watch the Queen on her route from Thornton Manor, where she stayed overnight as the guest of Lord and Lady Leverhulme, to Laird's Birkenhead shipyard. Just as the royal car entered the shipyard, a salute of 21 guns was fired from the deck of HMS Illustrious. More than 2,500 Wallasey children saw the spectacular event from the ferryboats in the river. At a celebration lunch, the Queen said the Ark Royal was "a great and beautiful ship" and the fulfilment of the dreams of our most brilliant naval architects, "built by workers whose skill was unequalled. It is the most wonderful launch I have ever seen."

Ark Royal R09 was the first ship to be constructed with an angled flight deck and steam catapults, allowing aircraft to land and take off from the carrier at the same time. She went through two major overhauls, one in the late 50s and one in the late 60s.

A television documentary in 1976 showed a glimpse of life on board during her Western Atlantic deployment.

The motto of the iconic warship was 'Desire Does Not Rest', but she left service in 1978.

Queen Elizabeth (the Queen Mother) at the launch of the Ark Royal in 1950

Ark Royal in Gladstone Graving Dock, undergoing heeling trials to test her equipment when the ship is listing

Cammell Laird handover to the Royal Navy in 1955

"The Ark Royal was the fulfilment of the dreams of our most brilliant naval architects, built by workers whose skill was unequalled."

Steaming at speed in 1957

HMS Ark Royal leaves Liverpool
in 1970, pictured from Wallasey

Crew welcome Hawker's chief test pilot Bill Bedford, after he had made the first ever vertical landing by a jet on a carrier at sea, 1963

The compass platform on the bridge with its impressive array of dials and controls, 1955

A life on the ocean wave – crew during a visit to Liverpool in 1970

Four members of the old Ark Royal, which was sunk in the Mediterranean in 1945, seen aboard their new vessel at Birkenhead in 1955 – Lieut. Commander Keresley, Commander Fell, Captain Campbell and Lieut. Commander Wooletan

Laird workers wave 'bon voyage' to HMS Liverpool in 1980

KEEPING THE NATION AFLOAT

The golden years down on the Mersey banks, when Cammell Laird was the biggest employer in Birkenhead, is the way the Lairdsmen remember their careers – with affection for happy times

SURE, there were bad times as well. Shop stewards addressed huge meetings in the car park of the Royal Castle pub opposite the yard. Men raised their fists to strike.

But today it is the sense of achievement, from building some of the world's greatest ships, which they recall most vividly. The yard was huge and it was a community of men: the caulkers and carpenters, burners and riveters, riggers and blacksmiths, the sparkies and plumbers, the drillers and boilermakers, the platers, the welders.

Inside the pub, the barmaids laid out dozens of pint glasses half-filled with bitter in preparation for the lunch-hour rush. Most workers added a bottle of brown – the Birkenhead cocktail.

And of course they had those nicknames for each other. There were the Solicitors (Williams and Williams), the Barber, Rembrandt (keep us in the picture, will you?), the Watchmaker, the Cobbler, The Vicar (he's out every Sunday, him). One shipwright heard that his nickname was Jones the Pill. Well, what do you expect if you're a Welshman given the job of "berth planning manager"?

Night and day the sheds of the old yard throbbed to the sounds of men building the ships. Sweat rolled from their brows and hammers thundered on rivets, each one inching into steel.

Sirens screeched, hooters blared, water lapped against the quays, wind whistled across the scaffolding and those red-hot rivets sizzled in buckets of water, ready to secure their ships.

This was the orchestra of industry.

More important than that, though, were the ships launched from the yard and their names read like a glorious chapter in Royal Naval history, as, indeed, they were.

But with the end of the war came new competition from all over the world as the new global economy led to a decline in orders. During the 1960s and 1970s, the company suffered as the shipbuilding industry began to decline.

By 1977 the yard had been nationalised, but it went back into private hands eight years later.

The last surface ship built was HMS Campbeltown in 1989, while the last complete boat to be built at the yard was the submarine HMS Unicorn in 1993.

"Night and day the sheds of the old yard throbbed to the sounds of men building the ships."

The team of launchway shipwrights who worked beneath the hull of HMS Liverpool

Shipyard workers salute the launch of type 42 Destroyer HMS Edinburgh, April 1983

Apprentices Michael Judge and Alan Norman checking the level of the decking on a project in 1982

In 1981 Cammell Laird received an order to build a drilling unit for offshore oil exploration. At that time it was the most valuable offshore contract obtained from abroad for a British yard, marking the start of a new era for Laird's. Standing at a massive 109 metres, Sovereign Explorer was handed over in 1983

HMS Coventry was laid down by Cammell Laird in 1973 and launched in 1974. She was accepted into service in 1978, seen here, leaving the River Mersey

HMS Campbeltown, a type 22 frigate, was launched on October 7, 1987, by Lady Kathleen Fitch

"With the end of the war came new competition from all over the world...The last surface ship built was HMS Campbeltown in 1989."

Children wave goodbye to
HMS Campbeltown in 1987

The cranes were the symbol of the Mersey's ship-building prowess.
Below, the workforce gather for a Union Meeting in 1990

GLAS
TEMS
KEEP CAMMELL LAIRD AFLOAT - 051 64

Cammell Laird appeal for help on the board donated
to them for the televised cup game at Anfield, 1991

The trade union campaign to save the Cammell Laird shipyard
received a marketing boost in 1990 with the introduction of
a new logo. 1,000 posters bearing the seven-bladed ship's
propellor design were printed and displayed on prominent
public buildings all over Merseyside. The seven blades showed
the initials of the seven unions represented at Laird's, with
those of the coordinating CSEU on the central hub.
Left, ship workers Keith Steele and George Murray
contemplate the sale of the shipyard in 1990

NEW HORIZONS

Cammell Laird remains one of the most illustrious names in British industry

TODAY, the Birkenhead firm has a 120 acre site with four dry docks, a modular construction hall and 40,000m2 of covered workshops. The company specialises in military ship refit, commercial ship repair, upgrade and conversion and heavy fabrication and engineering in the civil nuclear and energy sector. Cammell Laird deals with a wide variety of projects ranging from specialist offshore conversions and fabrication, commercial ship-repair through to the refit and upgrade of highly complex naval auxiliaries.

In both 2009 and 2010 the company pumped more than £30m into the Merseyside economy and more than £44m into its UK supply chain. In 2010, the company employed more than 1500 workers in full time and contracted positions.

Managing Director John Syvret of Cammell Laird in Birkenhead looks forward to a busy future

Today the company also employs more than 80 apprentices and recruits 11 more every nine months. In June 2010 the National Apprenticeship Service named Cammell Laird's apprentice programme one of the top three in the region for large employers at an awards ceremony in Manchester.

In June 2009 the company was named Business of the Year at the Liverpool Daily Post 'North West Business Awards' at St George's Hall. The award was accepted by the firm's founder and Chief Executive John Syvret.

The work is a split between military and commercial contracts. In June 2008 the company signed its biggest single contract in seven years with the Ministry of Defence.

The contract, worth nearly £1bn over more than 25 years, sees Cammell Laird provide 'through life maintenance support' to 11 ships in the Royal Fleet Auxiliary (RFA) in the UK and around the world. The contract is reviewed every five years.

In August 2010 Cammell Laird began a £40m three year contract to build the flight decks for the new Queen Elizabeth II class aircraft carrier for the UK Ministry of Defence.

Cammell Laird is ideally located to undertake commercial marine work. Each year the company completes around 70 commercial contracts from its Mersey base. The contracts mainly focus on drydocking, upgrades, refits and maintenance. The vessels worked on include tankers, ferries, dredgers, tugs and off shore support ships. Key clients include: James Fisher Ltd, Stena Line Ferries, Caledonian McBrayne, Bibby Line and Norfolk Line.

The broad skill set at the business also enables it to undertake ship conversion work in the international marine market. In February 2010 the company completed a multi million contract to lengthen the Nexans Skaggerak, a Norwegian cable laying vessel.

This contract saw the yard construct a huge new 30m wide midsection and lengthen the ship from 106.00m to 118.5m.

Cammell Laird – Illustrious is the word...

"The broad skill set at the business enables it to undertake ship conversion work in the international marine market."

GOLDEN MEMORIES OF GLORY DAYS

The life of a Lairdsman...

EVERYONE knew that Birkenhead built great ships in that yard, a short walk upstream from the priory, where the 12th-century Benedictine friars had begun ferrying merchants across the Mersey to Liverpool.

A proud and skilled town, Birkonians could stare across the Mersey to the glamorous buildings of the Liverpool waterfront knowing that they, too, had made history.

The shipyard gave the town so much of its culture – a wonderful brass band and choir, sporting teams and other societies. And life was so interesting at the yard. There was a story to every ship...

Apprentices share a joke in 1990

Despite the presence of a heavy hydraulic
hammer, it still took four men to hammer
this steel plate into shape for the stern
door of a tanker, 1950s

"It was hard, heavy work. We made rough forgings,
including propellor shafts and shaft coupling bolts...
The yard was working flat out. At one stage three
submarines were being built on the slipway."
Ron Rule, Pensby

Workers leave the factory in the 1970s

"I was very happy there and we had a good crowd of lads. It was great to go on the slipway, see the keel being laid, the ship gradually taking shape and being launched into the wet dock, taking it out to sea on trials, and then handing it over to the owners. There was a great sense of pride in being Laird's men and in the end product."
Greg Dawson, Irby

The prow of Laird's King Orry, looms over shipyard workers in 1975

"I worked on Manxman and her five earlier sister ships, starting with King Orry in 1945, and was a bit weary by the time we finished. I watched Manxman being launched on a grim, grey day in February, 1955. It was a heart-stopping experience, having put every plate together like a giant Meccano set."
Harry Mooney, Winsford

"There was one time when we were going to launch a tanker and it was so cold that the grease was freezing. They had 50-gallon oil drums full of fire all around the ship trying to keep it warm enough. Eventually we did, after about three days."
Bob Hunt

Ice almost covers the Mersey near the Birkenhead shore in 1947 – a picture taken from the Birkenhead Stage looking up the river to the Cammell Laird yards

A submarine section being moved into the construction hall in October 1987

"The yard was very busy building warships, mainly S and A class submarines and destroyers in 1944. I enjoyed watching the launches. Some of the ships were launched by foremen and managers as they were getting built so quickly. "
Geoff Moore, Upton

The awesome structure of a 350-foot submersible oil rig being built at the shipyard in the 1980s

Raising a glass at Cammell Laird Sports Club

CAMMELL LAIRD SPORTS CLUB

"The crane wasn't the easiest thing to drive, it took a while to get used to it. But once I got going, I was working on warships, cruise liners and cargo boats. You name it we could build it."
Billy Suckley, Bebington

"There was a chap who mended watches in his hut, whenever he had a moment free from his duties. One day a crane driver brought in his watch. The repairer soon had it ticking. But the following day it stopped again. The crane driver returned. The repairer said he would have another look at it. When the watch was finally working, he asked the crane driver for another two shillings. The crane driver was very annoyed and threw the money at him. That afternoon he got up on the crane and dropped his hook down on the hut with the watch repairer in it and knocked it about six feet up the quay. The man and all the bits on his shelves ended up in a big heap on the floor. We all thought that was hilarious."
Jim Irlam, West Derby

Keeping the ship shipshape – HMS Liverpool, 1980. Dennis Coady and his team

GREAT READS FROM THE HEART OF THE CITY

SCOTTIE ROAD

The bricks and mortar of Scottie Road may be a memory but the spirit lingers on. Featuring great photographs from the Scottie Press collection and rarely seen historical images from the League of Welldoers' Lee Jones Collection

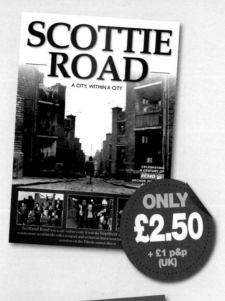

ONLY £2.50 + £1 p&p (UK)

ONLY £2.50 +£1 p&p (UK)

THE WAY WE WORKED

Unilever, Vernons, Littlewoods, Crawford's, Tate & Lyle, Woolies. Our jobs – our memories

NEW BRIGHTON OUR DAYS OUT REMEMBERED

Recall magical childhood summers of the golden era of what was the greatest seaside resort in the whole world

ONLY £3.99 +£1 p&p (UK)

ONLY £3.99 +£1 p&p (UK)

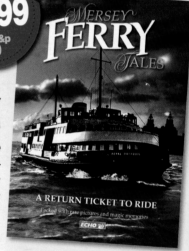

MERSEY FERRY TALES

A ticket to ride on the world's most famous ferry – a unique collection of magic maritime memories

LOST CINEMAS OF LIVERPOOL

Book your ticket for a trip down movie memory lane, to a time when Liverpool was a Tinsel Town in its own right and there was a cinema on every corner

ONLY £3.99 +£1 p&p (UK)

THE LOST TRIBE OF EVERTON & SCOTTIE ROAD

This nostalgic book by Ken Rogers will take you back 'home' into the inner city streets and make you feel proud

ONLY £9.99 FREE p&p (UK)

Offers while stocks last. Prices subject to change. Please telephone for international shipping rates.

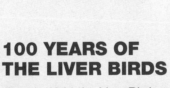